Adolescent Musings on a Monday Afternoon

Hannah Sedlak

BookLeaf
Publishing

India | USA | UK

Presentation by *BookLeaf Publishing*

Web: www.bookleafpub.com

E-mail: info@bookleafpub.com

ISBN: 9789357445962

First edition 2022

ACKNOWLEDGE MENT

I'd like to thank my fiancé, Jake, for knowing the words to say to calm me in times of turmoil; my eldest sister, Liz, for being an advocate for me when I have trouble standing up for myself; my elder sister, Rebecca, for editing my writing and teaching me basic punctuation when we were young; my mother, Roberta, for loving me unconditionally; my father, Rick, for being the best man I have ever known; my friend, Todd, for encouraging me to go after what I want; my friends, Rachel and Holly, for being ears to vent to and shoulders to lean on through our years of finding ourselves; my step-daughter, Juniper, for teaching me the meaning of motherhood; and all the boys I've ever loved–you know who you are.

PREFACE

The majority of this work was written a little over 10 years ago during my senior year of high school. My poetry phase at that time was instigated by undiagnosed depression, high school romance (or lack-there-of), and the annually assigned Shakespearean dramedy. Having a penchant for creative endeavors, I'd tried my hand at poem-writing over the years, usually at the behest of teachers or in fulfillment of classroom assignments, but this bout was different; the agony overflowed and needed an outlet, so the words I wrote, imbued with meaning, dripping in subtext. This was my therapy: the closure I sought to paradoxes I was powerless to. The darkness within these pages is simply an expression–like of a wound–of the mind, complete with blood and pus and torn skin. And as "this mortal coil" has become easier to bear, the wounds have healed, though the scar tissue may be tender yet.

In short, I'm an average human being who sometimes gets a little too sad and likes to make wordplay to feel better. This is simply an amassing of those attempts at self-help. Teenage (and adult!) angst is fickle. Growing up is hard.

Much love,

Hannah

DEDICATION

For Hannah, age 17-27

Lonely in Suburbia

Sometimes the wind blows in the dark,
And rain, it whispers to a stop.
The land drinks up the water of sky
And stars then shine and glisten and sigh
From ground, their prison of earthly bonds,
Entrapped and caught: a love without song.
And gone come morning and burning sun–
A power too great and freedom none,
A god controlled by nature's will,
As little choice as the lights it kills.
And gone they are and gone they'll be
'Til night restarts its symphony.
A shudder, a crack, a moan, a spark,
And then the wind blows in the dark.

How sweet the Flowers Fall

How sweet the Flowers Fall For thee,
How Humble in their dainty dance.
their lightness and Fragility
does Hold the eyes but For a glance.

and though Harsh death of Humankind
Hath pluckt them For its selfish schemes
they live Here on in purpose mind,
on Fingers soft, on bed of dreams.

How Happy do the Flowers Fall,
their life now giv'n on joyous day,
and catch the Feet and love the Hall,
How Happy do the Flowers lay.

and when they're crisp with brittle bones
Happy they'll be to Have but Flown.

Crushed Ice

Perspiration meanders
I fan myself with my paperback
Ice clinks
Lemonade sweet
Straw sputters at the bottom

You arrive

Two tables over
The crack of the newspaper
We pretend to read
Stealing glances greedily
Five weeks the same routine

Yet today's escapade
Suddenly ceased
By an interruption of blue: your wife

I leave my payment
My glass
My anticipation

Yet
In passing table
Elbow brushes shoulder

Apologies gasped
And finally
We meet

A touch
A smile
I float away
Filled with something sweeter
Than lemonade

Amariel

Of darkened thorns and jagged stains of moss,
A sanctuary torn, forgotten now.
The ruins cracked, a spider's web of gloss
Surrounds the mouth where naked sinners bow,
Or once they did, but now they do not stand,
Mere skeletons with skeletonic hearts;
All flesh has melted off their bones, and land
Has drunk and tasted sun and fear and dark–
A toxic poison, strong of seed and milk,
The essence made of bare humanity,
Intrudes the ground, infects it with its filth,
And kills the rose with infertility.
The lethal drug of life lives on inside
The gates of this dark land for you to find.

Collarbones

The subtle curves and gentle slopes intrigue
While shadows dance and swim along your
bones
Stretched tight, apparent in your light fatigue
The softest nude, the loveliest of shades

Bells Unrung

Your whispers are so dark inside
They gleam and shimmer and catch my eye
Deep pools of empty, bliss, and calm
A warming touch on nights of long
A soothing stroke, a whetted tongue
Far echoes of our bells unrung
So soft and silent, cool and clean
The peace of heart, the scent of green
And lay I here in your dark words
This refuge from a fallen world
Keep out the day, keep out the light
Let only in the breath of night
And come inside your world of dark
And let us melt our naked hearts

Pining for Our Impossible Future

It will pass
It will pass
And yet the liver yearns
For that which gives it breath
If these honest lies are his truth
And the manic images
Self-seeking
Of salvation
Like two rays
Are imperfect representations
Of the fifth dimension
Why won't it cease?

Unrequited

Lonely as a hawk, I watch
Feet growing numb
Toes prickle
Flesh melts from my bones
He sits near, silent
Except for the turning of a page
The crisp separation of thinly pressed wood pulp
The flap as it falls into place
A rustle
His jacket moves against his skin
His finger–a bobbing jay–
Silent, solemn, subtle
Restless
Adjusting a strap
Tracing a lip
Mine part
And yet, to me, he gives not a look
Is unrest contagious?
No, for wires trail to his temples
Music is his muse

XXX

In the forest, among the trees
I try and hide my humble leaves.
A fear of knowledge and of courtship
Led me here to taste the rose hips.
Bitter? Sweet? My senses numb.
I cannot speak, for I am dumb.
My screams and cries I cannot utter,
Though other trees can moan and mutter.

Whisper they do as you draw near,
Creeping slowly on my frontier.
What malice is this in your motive
Or desire you think you can give?
And yet I open my leaves to you
And let you drink of my morning dew.
A breath, a kiss, I breathe you in
And feel the eyes of my jealous kin.
You hold, you cherish, in dark and rain,
And then a knife you do proclaim.
You carve in me a word–your name.
At first my heart, and then I came,

Though just to please and to appease you.
Yet you of men I thought were few,
For no one can give here to trees:

Our branches brambled, our feet ugly,
Our bark is rough and oft misshapen
And when we love it leaves us shaken.
For no one can give here to roots
And mine are tall and trip your boots.
And you cannot give here to eyes,
Though mine are great, my only prize.

Yet then you complimented far
And won me over against my guard.
And with my fruit I fed and filled you,
You who spoke, and you who knew,
And you who let my branches bend
To give you life–the son of men–
And you, and you, and you again.
And you were who to whom I lent
These branches weak with thorns and thistles
And yet that night you gave them kisses.

I drank of you that night of dark
And in my blood you left your mark.
Pin up, bring down, "Relief," you say–
A crack in such a beautiful day.
And though to memories I cling,
I would not change a single thing.

i am your sweet bird
of happiness

a little bird
of broken shade
whose dark wings fade
and cries and heard
by ears employed,
indifferent and cruel.
her owner rules
and feeds–enjoyed–
on sweetened flesh.
the feathers stick
and make him sick;
their souls then mesh.
yet he knows not
and lets her little bird body rot.

What once was blossoming

Be there a rose of queer, peculiar hues
No pinks nor reds to be your dainty muse
But thorns usurp the glory of all views
And wrinkled leaves shine black with morning
dew
A color dark of wind with fatal news
And whisper trails that crawl with light of bruise
The darkened flow'r with broken stem abused
So plucked from ground and severed and
misused
With petals flung in dirt, no dressings left to lose
Abandoned without thought, empty as the
queues
And this ironic was the boy to choose
The rose of rare of which there are but few

The Side Effect of Dying

A troubled mind of dark and lonesome thought
Provides the bed in which a seed can sow
The false and tainted tendrils of a plot,
Too deep, too rooted now to overthrow
The pictures race like ticker tape, parades
No more–a happy place now bare and wrecked
Where rumination spoiled and decayed
What once was taut, now sagging with neglect
No gleam of hope, no whisperings of faith
A bleak despair encompasses the grey
Deep shadows pool, a bathtub drowned in
wraiths
A kiss of silver wet with hate and pain
Alas! A shimmer far? A beacon near?
It stands the final string to cut is fear.

Bragrilid

Bent, malformed, too small to see,
They writhe and beat and try to be free.
But stuck within, they rot and die,
'Til dried and black, they crumble inside.
And leave, they do, small sacks of death,
Brokenness, and blackened breath,
To spread disease and misery
And taint the bones and kill the breed.
And so to death she falls, they sing,
The bird-girl born with broken wings.

Passing Notes

I know now
the difference between
your blood and
my tears:

yours
eventually
runs dry

Things I Will Not Inherit

Baby clothes, 0-3 mo., 30 years old
School desk, mid-century
Beloved rings, now lost, not found
A mother's love

Metamorphosis

Remember:

the sun rises
and the sun sets;

caterpillars build cocoons and emerge
as butterflies;

tadpoles grow into frogs;

seeds bloom into flowers,
and flowers
morph
into fruit.

Beginnings.

Bending through hallways
Hoops to jump through
Applause
Fading
There are still stairs to climb
The stairway grows longer
But are you driven by the clapping of others
or the beating of your own heart?

Writer's Block

Race cars and freight trains
The thoughts behind my eyes dazzle and blind,
Dancing 'cross my lids on stars and comet tails
They swim in pools, impossibly black
And haunt my ever-conscious self with
universes unending
The infinite realm into which I spectate lies just
beyond
My fingertips brush
But inhibitions linger
The visions spurt by, signifying defeat:
Only dreams, never achievements
Inspiration vanishes
And I am alone.

Nineteen

"Nineteen and dreary," she states with a smirk,
"With autumn-colored hair and eyes of galaxies,
With freckles and fingers and twitches and
quirks,
With a head full of numbers and odd fantasies,

"With short legs and short arms and pasty pink
skin,
With itches and scratches and pimples and
pricks,
With lips far too red, with too small a chin,
With too short a torso, with thighs much too
thick,

"With fingernails bitten and paint chipped away,
With legs smooth as satin and still freshly
shaved,
And with a heart full of birds, vanilla, and gray,
And with maybe a tongue too much well
behaved."

Her eyes then drift off to her book-laden shelf
As she contemplates how she gave up the truth
of herself.

Forgiven

I take up space
The curve of my hip squeezes you out of your
comfort zone
My lungs are full
No tears to smear my makeup

Prickle knees
Fuzzy teeth
Cumin and lime are my marinade
Slime biscuit

"How high?"
How low,
To think my worth
Worthy of measurements

I forgive you
For ever thinking I was never enough
And too much
All at once

Courage (勇気)

それなのに
暗い夜でも
月がいる

Nevertheless, on
Even the darkest of nights
There still is the moon

* 9 7 8 9 3 5 7 4 4 5 9 6 2 *